Life Savers
FOR
WORKING MOTHERS

Elsa Houtz

HARVEST HOUSE PUBLISHERS
Eugene, Oregon 97402

LIFESAVERS FOR WORKING MOTHERS

Taken from:
THE WORKING MOTHER'S GUIDE TO SANITY

Copyright © 1989 by Havest House Publishers
Eugene, Oregon 97402

ISBN 0-89081-802-9

Printed in the United States of America.

1

Working Mother 101

Course #101: "How to Be a Working Mother"

◆

Prerequisites: Time Management I, II, and III; Juggling; Economics; History of the Universe; Advanced Trivia; Child Psychology; Adolescent Psychology; Adult Psychology; Abnormal Psychology; Logic; Argumentation and Debate; Business Administration; Food Science; Exotic Small Pets.

Course Description: An overview of the skills and training required for successful performance of the dual role of the mother who is also employed outside the home. Will examine such topics as: why dirty clothes always outnumber clean ones; the historical conflict between children and soap; how to avoid scheduling important meetings at work on the days you have peanut butter on your blouse; how to sound professional when answering telephone calls that begin, "Mom, you know that lizard I had?"

Okay, time for a pop quiz. Let's see how much you really know about being a working mother. Selecting one or more adjectives from the list provided, fill in the blank below:

"Being a working mother is a

_____ job."

character-building	heartrending
debilitating	intense
demanding	imaginative
dirty	impressive
disturbing	mind-boggling
exasperating	never-ending
excruciating	overwhelming
exhausting	rewarding
exhilarating	satisfying
fun	underpaid
frantic	underappreciated
frazzling	underestimated
fulfilling	varied
ghastly	victorious
healthful	wonderful
important	zesty

Whatever else it is, being a working mother is a difficult job (which wasn't on the list—who wrote this quiz, anyway?). It's doling out discipline and then wondering whether you have done the right thing; it's providing vast amounts of love, support, and encouragement, even when you don't feel like you have any to give; it's doing chores at 10 P.M. simply because they're there. It's watching a two-hour Little League game while the list of other things you need to be doing in your off-work time grows longer and longer.

That's why the expression "working mother" is so odd. Being a mother is work, period. It's happy work, sad work, satisfying work, exasperating work, tiring work, energizing work— but it's definitely work.

Some of us, though, for whatever reason, have another job besides being a mother. We work in offices or factories or schools or stores for 30 or 40 hours a week, and the statisticians classify us as having full-time jobs.

They're wrong, of course. We have two full-time jobs.

Of the two, the one for which we receive a paycheck is probably the easier one. The rules are pretty clear. There's someone there to tell us how to do the job. We know what time to show up and when to go home. When we make a mistake, we find out right away, and there are ways of gauging how well we're doing; we don't have to wait 15 years to find out whether we did a good job or not. Pretty simple compared to motherhood, isn't it?

Part of the problem is that no one gives us a fixed set of guidelines for being good mothers. One expert says "Let your children express themselves freely so you won't hamper their self-actualization" while another says "Children want strict discipline; it gives them a sense of security—so let 'em have it!" Trends in parenting techniques, unfortunately, change almost as much as fashions do, so unless we make some firm decisions about the kind of mothers we want to be, we may find ourselves being strict one year and lenient the next! Our children will need a manual just to keep up with our changing rules.

On top of these fundamental difficulties of being a mother, those of us who also work outside the home carry around some added baggage. First, of course, are the basic logistical problems of fitting two full-time jobs into one day-to-day life. That involves finding the time and energy to give your best in both jobs, and still have enough left over to send birthday cards to your relatives, attend your friends' baby showers, get your hair cut, pay your bills, and change the cat's litter box.

As if that were not enough, we also have to cope with the headlines. You know the ones—you can pick up a major newspaper or magazine on any given day and find them. Do you recognize these?

> *"New Study Shows Children of Working Mothers Can't Read"*

> *"Are Working Mothers Hurting Their Children?"*

> *"Day-Care Scandal Rocks Nation"*

> *"Toddler Cries, 'I Want Mommy to Come Home' "*

Make you feel wonderful, don't they?

To top it all off, there is the simple historical fact that no generation before ours has ever tried this. We can't look to history to find out how women in the past handled the "working mother" role, because it's a new societal phenomenon. We are the first, the pioneers, and charting new territories can be tough.

The day I ordered the cake for my son's ninth

birthday, I learned that my own approach to being a working mother had gotten out of hand.

I wanted a specially-made cake, one with a baseball player on it, since my son likes baseball. It was a Tuesday evening, and his birthday was Saturday. I was patting myself on the back for planning ahead. My usual style would be to rush to the bakery the night before and take whatever cake they had on hand, even if it said "Good Luck in Your Retirement."

I had spent the last few days making detailed plans for the birthday party; buying matching paper plates, cups, and napkins; dreaming up games that could be played in our limited yard; and in general doing a very fine all-out, traditional-mother birthday-planning job. All this was done, of course, in the spaces between nine-hour days at the office and the usual roster of household chores. I was determined to be living proof that a working mother could still put on a bang-up birthday party.

So there I was, standing at the bakery counter while a young girl in a crisp uniform searched through her book of cake designs for a baseball figure. "I thought I saw one in here," she said. Then "Right. Here it is."

It was perfect—a batter in a blue-and-white uniform with a red cap. I was delighted. One more mission accomplished.

"Great!" I told the girl, and she began to write up the order. She asked me how big a cake I wanted, and what flavor, and what color icing.

Everything was fine until she said, "Now, when did you want to pick it up?"

Pick it up? I hadn't figured that into my schedule. (The store was ten minutes from my house, so we were talking about a 20-minute task.)

Something in my brain shorted out. The computer in my mind flashed DISK FULL . . . INSUFFICIENT MEMORY . . . ERROR . . . ERROR. . . .

I had plotted every moment of my life between Tuesday and Saturday, calculating exactly how everything had to fit together so that I would be ready by the time the party was to begin. I figured out what things I needed to get done on my lunch hour and what I could do after work.

I hadn't allowed the 20 minutes for picking up the cake. I hadn't even thought about picking up the cake. All the careful planning, the errand-running, the careful scheduling of the last few days was crumbling before my very eyes. I wanted to cry. My husband had to work all Saturday morning, then come home and set up the porch and the yard for the party, so he wasn't going to have a spare 20 minutes either.

What was I going to do? Picking up the cake would throw off my whole schedule! It would jeopardize the whole project! There was no place to fit it in! It was impossible! *I couldn't pick up the cake!*

The bakery clerk waited patiently. I stood there at the bakery counter, teary-eyed, totally overwhelmed, totally incapable of answering her question, wondering if that's what it felt like to have a nervous breakdown. At a bakery counter. How humiliating.

Finally, as mothers do, I rallied. I managed to say, "Saturday morning."

But there was more.

"What time?" she asked.

Am I going to live through this? I wondered.

"Ten," I said. "Ten in the morning."

"Okay," she said cheerfully. "See you then."
She handed me the receipt for the order, and I
raced out of the store.

On the way home, I obediently heeded a stern
voice inside me that said, "Get a grip on yourself.
What's the big deal about a 20-minute trip to pick
up the cake?"

Then a nurturing voice took over. "You're
probably just overtired. You'll feel better about
things tomorrow."

They were both right, I told myself. But deep
down, I knew something was wrong, something
that didn't have anything to do with the birthday
cake. Something was wrong with the way I was
living my life, with the mother-image I was trying to live up to, with the roles I was trying to
play.

Once again, as mothers do, I rallied. I com-
pleted all the arrangements for the party, picked
up the cake Saturday morning, and Saturday
afternoon was the proud hostess of a very successful birthday party.

The following Monday, however, I didn't go to
work. Nor the following Tuesday, nor any day
that week. I told my office that I was sick and not
to call me. I even told my friends not to call me—
and when the phone did ring, I didn't answer it.
For most of the next five days I lay on the sofa in
my family room, under the gold-colored Indian

blanket from my mother's house, feeling infinitely alone, trying to figure out what I was doing wrong.

I had it all—job, home, family—so why did I feel like I was losing my mind? I was an intelligent, capable person, a successful executive who managed a large department efficiently. Why couldn't I manage my life better? Everything in my world was nice—nice house, nice child, nice husband, nice job, nice friends—but something inside me was not nice at all. Inside I was lonely, bruised, and hurting. I promised myself that before the week was out I would make some changes in the way I treated myself.

As a working mother, have you had a "birthday cake" experience—some task or event that was just one thing too many, a "last straw" that made you feel you couldn't cope any longer? Did it make you question whether you could—or even wanted to—continue juggling your many responsibilities?

We work. We try our best to be good mothers. We nurture. We support. We meet other people's needs. And amid all the doing and going and being and pleasing and running, we seldom find ways to refresh our own spirits, to restore our own self-esteem, to acknowledge our own value as persons—*as persons*, not just as employees or mothers or some other role we play. Finding those ways to reaffirm ourselves is, I believe, a vital part of maintaining equilibrium and perspective in our lives. It's the key to staying sane in the crazy world of the working mother.

2

The Three G's: Guilt, Guilt, and Guilt

✦

I-Should-Be-Doing-Something-Else Guilt

When Kathy started running a few years ago, she just did it because she wanted to get some exercise and take off some extra pounds. She had a few friends who were serious runners who would run six or seven miles before they went to work in the morning, but she didn't have any plans that ambitious.

Before long, though, Kathy began to find that running did a lot more for her than just burning off calories. The exercise itself made her feel great. She felt healthier and more energetic, and was happy to notice that her clothes fit a little better. Someone at work even commented that she was looking especially trim lately.

Kathy liked both the early-morning run, when the air was fresh and the sun was just coming up, and the evening run, when she could feel the day's accumulated stress draining off with each step. She enjoyed the sense of accomplishment she felt each time she increased her distance, knowing she had built up greater endurance and strength.

Another benefit was that she made some new friends. She discovered some other women in her neighborhood and at work who were runners, and often arranged to run with one or more of them.

However, in the best tradition of working-mother guilt, Kathy often wondered whether she was being selfish. After all, she was devoting several hours a week to her running instead of spending that time with her family or at home catching up on housework. Often the enjoyment and satisfaction she got out of her running was spoiled by the guilt she felt when she thought about all the other things she could be doing with those hours. Should she be baking cookies instead of trying to top her distance record?

Kathy's inner conflict is typical of the way working mothers feel when they do enjoyable things just for themselves. Into our so-called "leisure time"—the hours we aren't at work—we have to squeeze housework, shopping, chauffeuring, and other chores, then hope we have time left to maintain the quality of family life and social relationships that we want.

Somewhere we have picked up the idea that as working mothers we have to "make up" in some way for the time we spend at work. Because our jobs require us to be away from our families 40 or more hours a week, we feel that *all* our nonworking hours necessarily have to be spent doing home-and-family things. The result: When we have a chance to treat ourselves to something just for fun or just because it's satisfying to us, we feel guilty. This is a hard habit to break.

Guilt, in general, implies some act of wrongdoing, some crime. Yet even when we haven't done anything wrong, we feel guilty! How can it be wrong to treat yourself like a person, giving yourself equal time to do the things you enjoy? For some reason, when it comes to ourselves, our sense of justice breaks down.

> *When the Bible tells us to be just and merciful, I think that must apply to the way we treat ourselves, too—not just the way we treat others. I think God wants us to be as fair to ourselves as we try to be to other people.* —Rolle

According to the Bible, God wants justice in His world. If He wants you and me to be fair and merciful in our treatment of other people, it stands to reason that He also expects us to treat ourselves the same way. How about deciding right now to reduce the amount of I-Should-Be-Doing-Something-Else Guilt in your life?

The next time you have a chance to do something for yourself, to treat yourself just for fun (assuming it won't break the bank or disrupt your family relationships!), try this: Instead of mentally listing all the reasons why it wouldn't be fair to your family for you to do it, try saying, "I give my family and my job my very best efforts. I give my family my love, my support, and my caring. I give my job my skills in the best way I know how. Now I'm going to give myself something!"

Can you do it? Good for you!

But-I'm-Superhuman Guilt

> *Give yourself a break.* —My mother

One day when my mother was visiting me, she asked me if I had finished something she had asked me to do earlier. I was feeling very pressured at the time and was under a lot of stress at work and at home, and I really didn't want any more pressure. I snapped at her. "No," I said irritably, "I haven't done it! I've had about a million other things on my mind and I just haven't gotten around to it!"

I don't know about you, but I was taught from day one to be respectful toward my parents. I was horrified at the way I had spoken to my mother. But she wasn't. When I apologized later, she said, "Forget it. You're only human. Nobody but you expects you to be perfect, you know."

Her loving acceptance of my behavior was very reassuring and relieved the guilt I felt at having spoken unkindly to her. I realized later, though, how accurate her observation was. I do expect myself to be perfect, and when I'm not, I feel guilty.

> If we confess our sins, he is faithful
> and just and will forgive us our sins . . .
> (1 John 1:9).

The Bible is filled with examples of forgiveness. God is always ready to forgive us; we have only to ask Him. If He can forgive us, surely we can forgive ourselves.

When we forgive someone, we put their guilt behind us, and we forget about it. We don't hold it against them or berate them over and over for what they have done. If they have been inconsiderate or forgetful or even unkind, we can simply accept it as human behavior, forgive and forget, and go on with the relationship.

But how do we treat *ourselves* when we make a mistake?

How many times have you poured But-I'm-Superhuman Guilt on yourself? Like when you have just come home from work, fatigued and frazzled, and your two-year-old dumps his chocolate milk on the carpet? You lose your temper, you raise your voice, maybe even paddle him—and then mentally punish yourself the rest of the evening.

Or when your husband needs to wear his best suit for an important job interview and you said you would pick it up from the dry cleaners, but then the night before the interview you simply run out of time and when he reaches for it, it's not there?

None of us likes to let down those who depend on us. We hate to forget things that are important to our loved ones. It hurts us when we are harsh or unfair to our children. We could kick ourselves around the block when a family birthday or anniversary goes by and we haven't sent the card we meant to get. But it happens. It just happens. We're human. Our resources of patience, understanding, energy, time, and ability to juggle our many responsibilities are limited, no matter how hard we try to stretch them to infinity.

Let's be more reasonable about our expectations of ourselves. If we know there's no way we can pick up that suit at the cleaners, let's say so and make some other arrangement. If we snap at a child or spouse, let's apologize to them and then forgive ourselves, knowing it's bound to happen from time to time. If the house isn't straight out of *Better Homes and Gardens* all the time, so be it. Let's set some priorities we are comfortable with and stop criticizing ourselves for our failures.

Human beings make mistakes. Let's follow the example of forgiveness God gives us, not just in forgiving others but in forgiving ourselves.

> Be kind and compassionate to one another, forgiving each other, just as in Christ God forgave you (Ephesians 4:32).

No-Win Guilt

Being a working mother is great as long as your kids stay healthy. —Dianne

Jill, a single mother who works full-time as a travel agent, told me a good story about No-Win Guilt. When her three-year-old daughter came down with the chicken pox, Jill naturally missed several days of work, since she had to stay home with her daughter.

When she returned to work the following week, one of her clients welcomed her back by saying, "Been having a little vacation, eh?"

"It was all I could do to keep from laughing," Jill told me later. "Imagine—taking care of a three-year-old with the chicken pox a vacation? Hardly! I was glad to get back to work!

"The whole time I was at home with Amy, I kept thinking I should be at work, and it made me feel guilty. After all, I wasn't sick myself. I could have been working. And yet, I had to stay with her; there just wasn't anyone else to take care of her. It's my job."

If we're at work, we feel guilty because we're not at home with our children. If we're at home with our children, we feel guilty because we're not at work. Talk about a no-win situation!

No-Win Guilt has the same earmarks as the two other kinds of guilt: treating ourselves unjustly and creating unrealistic expectations.

Realistically now, how can we be in two places at once? And how fair is it to let ourselves feel guilty because we're only one person, not a clone that can be duplicated as the situation demands?

Try this: Make a commitment to allow justice and forgiveness for yourself. Be alert to your own—and other people's—unrealistic expectations, and identify them as such. Try to be more tolerant of your own human mistakes, while you work at improving on your weaknesses. As you make efforts to be fair and understanding to others, extend that same generous spirit to yourself!

How's Your Guilt IQ?

How much of an expert on guilt are you? Take this little quiz to find out. For each statement below, indicate whether it reflects:

#1: *I-Should-Be-Doing-Something-Else Guilt*

#2: *But-I'm-Superhuman Guilt*

#3: *No-Win Guilt*

After you've identified the kind of guilt, decide what you would do to deal with it.

_____ "Why do the dirty socks always outnumber the clean ones, even the day after I do the laundry? My family never seems to have any clean clothes. Guess I should drop my aerobics class and do laundry on Tuesday nights instead."

_____ "If I don't go to the fifth-grade Christmas party, my son will be the only child there without a parent. His teacher might think he's an orphan."

_____ "I really should cook more. My kids will grow up thinking 'home-cooking' is food you pick up somewhere and take home to eat."

_____ "Just once, instead of coming home from work and having three or four people clamoring for my attention and wondering what's for dinner,

I would like to come home to an empty house, put a frozen dinner in the oven, and read a book. Guess that's pretty selfish, huh?"

_____ "I should be thankful for what I have and not complain just because I have so much to do. What a terrible, ungrateful person I am."

Congratulations! You receive a grade of A+ on this quiz—just for taking it. There are no right or wrong answers; it's just a way to get you thinking about the many kinds of "I'm guilty" statements we make, either verbally or in our heads. Listen to yourself in the coming week, watching for "I'm guilty" statements—statements you actually express to someone else, or ones you make to yourself. When you hear one, decide what you want to do about it.

1) Determine whether you've really done anything wrong. As we discussed earlier, guilt implies wrongdoing.

Not long ago when I was in charge of a meeting at work, my watch stopped and the meeting ran a half-hour longer than it was supposed to. As a result, several of the people involved were late for another meeting right afterward, which was a major inconvenience to them and to the other people at that second meeting. I felt terribly guilty that I had let the meeting run over and caused them to be late.

Then, the more I thought about it, the more I could see how ridiculous it was to declare myself guilty of the "crime" of letting my watch stop. I hadn't done anything wrong—so I chose not to give in to guilt. (That was one of my more victorious encounters with guilt; I don't always win!)

2) Ask yourself whether you need to take some action to eliminate the cause of the guilt. Can you "fix" whatever it is you feel guilty about, or at least make a good-faith effort to improve or correct the situation? If that's practical and feasible, do it. If it will make you feel better to tell your toddler you're sorry for being cross and give him a hug, do it, rather than feeling guilty for the rest of the evening.

3) Make a decision not to just let guilt "ride." Don't carry it around. If there's no action you can take to remedy the situation, then simply drop the matter from your mental file. Guilt that we store away tends to build up and resurface later.

You might even try to picture in your mind some way of disposing of that particular "piece" of guilt. Imagine yourself rolling it into a ball and throwing it into the trash, or tying it to a helium balloon and letting it float away.

Like so many things, guilt will make us miserable if we let it. On the other hand, it can help us take constructive action. Guilt's only value lies in its ability to motivate us to act or cause us to reflect on some aspect of our thinking or behavior.

The better we understand God's concept of

justice, the better we can distinguish between guilt that prompts positive change and guilt that simply leads us to needlessly punish ourselves.

3

Expectations: Great and Not-So-Great

◆

Recently my 11-year-old son and I had a conversation about what we were doing for dinner that night. It went like this:

Matthew: "Mom, can we eat out tonight?"

Me: "No, not tonight, because I'm fixing a nice dinner here at home."

Matthew: "Oh." (Pause) "What are we having?"

Me: "Pork chops, peas, blueberry muffins, and a fruit salad, I think."

Matthew: "Oh." (Longer pause) "C'mon, Mom, can't we have a real dinner?"

Unconventional thinker that I am, I had expected that the meal I had described would qualify as a "real" dinner, but obviously it didn't in Matthew's book. So I pursued it.

Me: "What do you mean by a 'real dinner'?"

Matthew: "You know, one where we all fix our own stuff."

Me: "Oh."

So much for expectations.

— ◆ —

My mother is an enthusiastic and creative cook. When I was growing up, dinnertime was the family's time to be together, and there was always a balanced, appealing dinner on the table. We ate it without hurrying, regardless of how much homework there was or how many other tasks needed to be done afterward. We ate out only as a special treat.

Later on, my expectation of what dinnertime would be like in my own household was based on what I experienced as a child. My definition of a "real" dinner, historically, has been one that includes the four basic food groups, has a variety of colors and flavors, and is served in serving dishes, not in plastic containers that say "Serve by August 19." And you eat it sitting down at the table. Your body, your plate, your silverware, and your food do not leave the table until everyone has finished.

As you can imagine, the reality of dinnertime at my house has crashed head-on into this notion about how it should be. First of all, we seldom all sit down at the table at one time. Secondly, when we do eat at home, the meal generally takes about 45 minutes to fix and 15 to eat. (There's something mathematically wrong with that.) Invariably, the telephone rings while we're eating, and whoever the call is for finishes talking right about the time the others finish eating.

Sometimes we don't sit at the table at all. I have been known to fix the food, put it on the table with a stack of plates and utensils, and let each person eat whatever he wants, wherever he wants to. Another alternative, of course, is the one Matthew defined as a "real" dinner: the arrangement in which I announce that it's dinnertime and everyone fixes what he wants to eat. The four basic food groups at my house are: things that come in cans, things that don't, things that are frozen, and Twinkies.

Deep down in my heart, I know there's nothing wrong with any of these mealtime arrangements. (Well, maybe the four food groups are a little off-base.) They work for us. Our lives are busy and full, and we would rather do other things than linger over dinner. And certainly I would rather do other things than spend hours cooking. The way my mother approached dinnertime worked for those years and for the lifestyle our family had. The meal system in my household works for the way we live now.

> *I remember sitting around the dinner table when I was growing up, having long discussions about politics or books or sports or current events. It wasn't unusual for us to stay at the table for two hours or more. It scares me that that kind of family life might be gone forever.*
> —Patricia

But there is a part of me that remembers the traditional dinners in my mother's home and expects the same of me. It whispers that if I were a good mother, dinners in my home would be like that, too. It's an irrational and even silly expectation, but for some reason, when I fail to live up to it, it hurts.

What Do You Expect?

Unreasonable expectations not only cause us unnecessary hurt, frustration, and conflict, but they can also rob us of the freedom God wants us to have. They can limit our ability to develop fully the unique potential He has created in each of us. They bind us to thinking and behavior that don't fit the people we are.

Where do these unrealistic and inappropriate expectations come from? It's difficult to pinpoint all the sources, and certainly we could simply say that our expectations are shaped by "society." But let's be a little more specific, and look at three particular sources of expectations about what working mothers should be: personal history, the media, and other people.

"And the Rest Is History"

The mismatch between my expectations and reality in regard to dinnertimes is a reflection of the difference between my life as a child and my life now, between how my mother fulfilled her role and how I fulfill mine. It is unrealistic and foolish for me to think that I can simply transplant my mother's lifestyle into today and proceed as though nothing had changed in the past 30 years. Given the pace and the extent of change in our time, the idea of simply transplanting our mothers' lifestyle and way of doing things into this radically different world seems ludicrous. Yet many of us try in varying degrees to do just that. We try to fulfill our role as mothers in the same way the previous generation did. Then we add on another full-time job outside the home.

In other words, we try to do all those things that, based on history, we think mothers ought to do. Then on top of this schedule we spend eight or ten hours a day somewhere else, living up to a whole different set of expectations in the workplace. What a burden to take on!

How do we resolve the conflict, then, between these expectations stemming from our personal history and the realities of our daily lives? By setting priorities and making choices.

Let's go back to the dinnertime situation. I've talked with many other mothers who experience the same discrepancy between mealtimes they knew as children and the ones in their households now, and they want to find some way to relieve the inner tension that this causes. What are our options? Here are a few:

1) We can decide that being together at dinnertime is going to be a priority in our family's lifestyle. In that case, we need our family to make a collective commitment. Adults and children alike need to avoid scheduling activities at dinnertime. Phone calls received during the meal should be returned after dinner. If we want dinnertime to be a meaningful, pleasant family time together, then it cannot be used as a dumping ground for the day's frustrations, or as a time to discipline, scold, or punish children.

2) If it's not the "family dinner" tradition that is our priority as much as simply having relaxed, pleasant times of being together, then we need to find other opportunities to build those times into our lives. Some families enjoy going to the movies together, or to the beach, or on weekend

picnics in the park, or spending Sunday afternoons at the home of good friends. Just because leisurely, sit-down dinners are a rarity at our house doesn't mean we have failed to build a sense of family togetherness. It's the *time* that counts, not the setting and not the food.

3) Compromise. Maybe we can all sit down to dinner together on Wednesday nights and Sunday afternoons, or on any two nights during the week, depending on activities. Maybe each family member will be responsible for "organizing" dinner on a different night and surprising the rest of the family with a special menu. Or maybe every other Sunday one of the children gets to suggest an activity he or she would like the family to do, even if it's just watching a rented video together or baking cookies.

If our dinnertime or our family life or our leisure time together isn't what we want it to be, that is probably because we haven't made a commitment to what we do want it to be. The quality of our life as a family stems from the choices we make. External forces shape that quality only when we allow them to. If we don't make choices that will bring about the quality of life we want, then by default we are letting the rest of the world make those choices for us.

The Keys to Success:
Mouthwash, Cheese, and Low Heels

Living as we do in the "information age," we are constantly bombarded with messages that feed this schizophrenic way of life. Magazines, books, newspapers, movies, TV shows, and advertising all portray women in a variety of ways and give us plenty of instruction about what we ought to be doing and how. To get a glimpse of society's expectations for working women, mothers, working mothers, and women in general, we need only to look to the images created by the media.

From my own observations, here are a few of the messages about working mothers you can find in the media on any given day:

✦ If you buy a certain brand of peanut butter, milk, mayonnaise, cheese, or toilet paper, your family will know you love them.

✦ Having clean, fresh-smelling clothes is of paramount importance to your loved ones. It's the least you can do for them.

✦ Having clean, fresh-smelling carpets is of paramount importance to your loved ones. It's the least you can do for them.

✦ Never appear in public unless you are fully made up and wearing clothes that match. Your "I Climbed Pike's Peak" T-shirt and University of Tulsa running shorts do not constitute an ensemble.

✦ Your hairdo should last all day. So should you.

✦ If you are overtired, or have the flu, or sprain your ankle, that's no reason to slow down. Just take XYZ pharmaceutical products and you'll be able to remain standing, and maybe even breathing, all day.

✦ Nothing hurts you. No demand on your time, energy, or emotion is too much. Nothing makes you sad or angry or frustrated. You can do anything. You're a working mother.

I think sometimes we let society and the media tell us what we should be doing. There's just so much information out there, and we buy into it without even being aware that we're doing it.
—Joan

In the last three weeks, not one but two women have told me what a hard decision it was for them to start wearing dresses to work instead of suits. These were both intelligent, capable, high-level professional women who were used to being in charge and making important decisions. Yet they had been so conditioned to the expectation that wearing a suit at work was somehow related to success that they had to wrestle with the decision to wear something else instead. They had bought into the stereotype of the business-suited successful woman, perhaps without even being aware of it, and had to make a specific decision to break out of that pattern. To be honest, I was proud of them both for declaring their freedom from the suit-up-for-success syndrome!

Are there any stereotypes or unrealistic images that have sneaked into your thinking and influenced your behavior? Do you need to break out of some pattern you have let enslave you? Our roles as mothers, our working lives, and our self-concepts are too important to let someone else define them for us.

Okay, Have It Your Way

Another set of expectations about how we should live our lives comes from the people around us: friends, families, coworkers, church members, and people we perceive as authority figures or role models. Often, we may respect certain people's opinions or examples in one area of their lives—say, their religious beliefs or the way they conduct themselves on the job—and inadvertently buy into their views in other areas as well without really evaluating them.

Over the years, I have worked closely with a number of talented, dedicated professional colleagues, both men and women, whose work style and accomplishments I greatly admired. For me, these individuals set the standard. I wanted, above all, to be like them, to perform on the job as effectively and creatively as they did.

Over time, though, I realized that while I could learn a great deal from them—and did—I could never make the total career commitment they had made. The priorities in my life were different. My commitment was to a balanced life in which my career was one element, not the driving force. Family, church, recreation, and physical fitness were all priorities for me, too. A totally job-centered life just wouldn't leave enough room for the other things I wanted. I could never attain the things my colleagues attained because I wasn't willing to pay the price. I had to learn to be selective about what aspects of their lives I imitated in my own.

On the other hand, I have a number of good friends who simply do not believe that mothers of small children should hold jobs outside the home. They feel that a working mother is a less-than-adequate mother. There was a time when I let myself believe they were right, and that I must be a poor mother indeed to continue my job when I had a small child at home. I let my respect and love for these individuals produce a tremendous sense of guilt. And it was only because I was letting their opinions and beliefs—instead of my own—shape my expectations.

> *One of the things that's helped me a lot is giving myself the freedom to say, 'Sometimes I don't like being a mother very much.'' For some reason, a lot of people are afraid to admit that it isn't just great all the time. It's great most of the time—but we all have our moments. I like being free to admit that. —Ava*

Why are we so willing to adopt other people's expectations as our own, even when it's clear they are not right for us?

I believe one of the reasons is that we haven't

had much opportunity to establish our own definitions of who and what we ought to be. There's no historical track record that tells us what works and what doesn't. There's no road map with the potholes clearly marked. We are like inventors, trying out a new invention for the first time, with no data that tell us what to expect.

So it's up to us. We have to start from scratch, defining for ourselves how we are going to live.

"I'm A Designer Original!"

God created each of us lovingly and individually as a reflection of Him. He is continually interested in us and concerned for our well-being. We know He loves and cares about us. The Bible also tells us that He has given each of us a special combination of gifts—talent, personality, skill, ability—that equips us to fill a role in this world that no one else can fill. And that's the only role that really matters, because as we seek to fill that "master role," the other things we do will fall into place.

> So do not worry, saying "What shall we eat?" or "What shall we drink?" or "What shall we wear?" For the pagans run after all these things, and your heavenly Father knows that you need them. But seek first his kingdom and his righteousness, and all these things will be given to you as well. —Jesus (Matthew 6:31-33)

The people of Jesus' time were concerned about God's expectations of them. They asked

Jesus to tell them the most important things God wanted them to do. The answer He gave them is as true today as it was then. "Love the Lord your God with all your heart and with all your soul and with all your mind," He told them, and "Love your neighbor as yourself" (Matthew 22:37-39).

The Bible spells out God's expectations of us. He makes clear the kind of lives He wants us to live. When our focus is on being the *people* He wants us to be, then we will be the kind of mothers, workers, spouses, friends, and citizens He wants us to be also. No matter how many roles we fulfill, we will still be centered in His loving concern. I believe the ultimate freedom lies in that knowledge.

God's Expectations

Lord, what do You want me to do?

What are Your expectations of me?

To care about that old-fashioned idea called "righteousness";

To make my life choices and my day-to-day decisions with integrity and compassion;

To be truthful and constructive in the things I say, and not use the power of words to hurt other people;

To treat others fairly and respectfully, knowing You created each of them with love, just as You did me;

To recognize evil when I see it, and to follow the example of people who love and honor You;

To keep my promises, both to You and to other people, even when it's hard to do;

To give of myself, my time, my talent, my resources generously, without demanding a high return;

Never to let the prospect of material or personal gain make me compromise what I know is right;

I know that if I do these things, nothing can conquer me, because You will sustain me.

(Based on Psalm 15.)

4

A Wise Choice

✦

When I was in my early 20's, I went to visit my godmother, who had moved to another state. Naturally, we had a great deal of catching up to do. We talked about her experiences and mine, and about growth and change and adversity. We both made a number of philosophical observations about life's trials and triumphs.

After we had talked for a while she said, "You know, you're very wise for a person your age."

Now, I am realistic enough to suspect that her words were those of a loving godmother who could see only the best in the godchild she had watched grow up. Nevertheless, even now, in my moments of discouragement and low self-esteem, I like to pull her words out of my memory bank and savor the knowledge that at least one person thinks I am wise. It gives me the confidence to believe that I can solve the problem at hand, that surely I can come up with an answer.

Wisdom is a precious commodity, and one that working mothers need in ample supply. We need wisdom to maintain balance. We need wisdom to make the numerous decisions we face every day, and to see past surface appearances into the hearts of people and situations. We need wisdom to manage the many relationships in our lives and to preserve a unified, focused sense of ourselves. We need wisdom to guide our children and prepare them for adulthood.

For me, wisdom is largely the ability to distinguish what is real from what isn't and what is important from what isn't. That is admittedly a simplistic definition, but even after much thought, it's the best I can do.

I'm not sure arriving at a dictionary definition of wisdom is essential anyway; I would rather explore the role it plays in our lives and, even more important, how we can increase our own wisdom.

Beyond the Limits

No matter how much education, skill, and experience we attain in our lives, the fact remains that human beings have limitations, and one of those is limited vision. The concept of infinity is outside our mental reach; our minds can grasp, process, and store only a finite amount of information. As a result, our view of any problem or circumstance is colored by our relationship to it, by our past experience, and by our beliefs and values. As my mother puts it, "It's what you see from where you sit."

God, on the other hand, has unlimited vision. He sees the entire universe at a glance. He sees the past, the present, and the future. He sees inside our hearts and minds.

"Oh, the depth of the riches of the wisdom and knowledge of God!" wrote the apostle Paul (Romans 11:33). Wouldn't it be terrific if we could somehow tap into that infinite, all-seeing wisdom God has? Wouldn't that make it easier to find our way through the maze of decision-making each of us faces, instead of blundering along on our own limited knowledge and insight?

Here's some good news:

> If any of you lacks wisdom, he should ask God, who gives generously to all without finding fault, and it will be given to him (James 1:5).

God promises to give us wisdom if we only ask. Doesn't that make it seem silly to struggle along, tormented by uncertainty and confusion, when unlimited wisdom is ours for the asking?

Of course, when we ask God for wisdom, we enter into a problem-solving partnership with Him, a team effort to address the questions and choices in our lives. Entering into this partnership commits us to two major responsibilities:

1. *When we ask God for wisdom, we must do so in the faith that we will receive it.* In the business world, the art of negotiating has become a highly sophisticated game of move and countermove. Often the basic strategy involved is: Ask for pie-in-the-sky, and then work down from there. It's like the teenager who comes up to his mother and says, "Mom, can I go to the Bahamas for the weekend with my friends?" Naturally, his mother says no, so he aims lower: "Then can I have the car Saturday night?"

That approach isn't the one God wants us to use in seeking His wisdom. We aren't to enter into negotiations by asking for something we would never expect to receive. He wants us to ask, believing wholeheartedly that He'll respond.

2. *We must be willing to be guided by His principles.* When we enter into this problem-solving

partnership with God, we are agreeing to play
by His rules. If we ask God for wisdom, we must
be willing to make decisions based on His stan-
dards of right and wrong, not on financial advan-
tage, ego needs, convenience, popular opinion,
what our friends think, or any of the many other
forces that might pressure us to choose other
options.

In this partnership, then, how does God give
us wisdom? How do we tap into His wisdom to
shape our decisions and perspectives?

Through Prayer

Prayer can help bring a problem into focus.
When we ask God for guidance, we lay out the
problem in prayer. As we do so, we put it into
words in our own minds, which in itself is use-
ful.

In addition, prayer reassures us that we
are not alone. By the very act of praying, we
acknowledge that Someone whose wisdom is
greater than ours is willing to share our burden
of decision-making.

Through the Written Word

God ordered the universe, then He gave us
guidelines for living in it. In the Bible He tells us
the things we need to know to function effectively and to be the people He intends for us to
be. "I am a stranger on earth," the psalmist
wrote; "do not hide your commands from me"
(Psalm 119:19).

When we make decisions guided by God's instructions, we draw on His wisdom rather than relying completely on our own limited vision and insight. The Bible even cautions us to "lean not on your own understanding" (Proverbs 3:5).

> Try this: Even if you are not a regular Bible reader, read the Book of Proverbs, starting at the beginning of chapter 10. Read a chapter or two a day for a week. As you read, consider the sound, down-to-earth advice those pithy little verses contain.
>
> Then the next time you face a difficult decision, read those chapters again, a few at a time, and at the same time ask God to help you apply them to the decision at hand. Let yourself be encouraged and inspired as you draw on the wisdom that has served mankind for thousands of years and yet is as pertinent and practical today as when it was written.

Through Other People

Throughout my adult life, my friends have been an invaluable resource of wisdom and insight. I remember one episode in which I was very angry and frustrated over something that had not gone the way I thought it should. I went storming into my friend Chuck's office and told him about it.

"Well," he said, "what do you think you can learn from this?"

At the time, I was a little irritated with him for not being more sympathetic and commiserating with me in my anger and disappointment. As I cooled off, of course, I realized his question was a valuable one, and as I looked back on the incident I was able to learn an important lesson. Many times since then, in the wake of disappointing experiences, I have asked myself that same question: What can I learn from this?

Sometimes hearing about another person's painful experience or unwise decision can help us avoid making the same mistake. Sometimes our friends see things we don't see when we're too close to a situation. And sometimes an offhand observation by someone else can start us thinking in a new direction and lead to a fresh insight.

Do You Hear What I Hear?

Jesus was a listener. From the many biblical accounts of His interaction with people, we can picture Him listening intently, focusing on the speaker, not cutting the other person off or giving a hasty reply.

Just think how much we can learn from listening carefully to other people, listening not only to what they are saying aloud but also to the underlying feelings, needs, and messages. So often in our fast-paced lives, we mentally rush on to the next subject or give an answer while a person is still speaking, and we miss the real meaning of what they are saying. If we could learn to be more patient and effective listeners, I believe we would take a major step toward greater wisdom.

As we look at Jesus as a listener, we need to bear in mind that He listened to God, too. God promises to give us wisdom if we ask—but we have to be listening when He answers.

Based on My Observations...

The young police officer was scrupulously polite as he wrote out a speeding ticket with my name on it, but that didn't relieve my embarrassment and anger with myself. He had stopped me for going 42 miles an hour in a 30 m.p.h. zone—in my own neighborhood. I felt humiliated by my lack of observation. How could I have missed the sign that changed the speed limit from 40 to 30?

It's expensive and embarrassing to miss a speed-limit sign. But when we get too out of touch with what's happening around us, we run the risk of missing something truly important. I think a prerequisite of wisdom is being observant about our environment.

Jesus was in touch with what was going on around Him. He repeatedly used examples from the everyday world to convey important spiritual truths. He compared faith to a tiny seed, or to building a house on rock instead of sand. He described faultfinding as looking at the speck of dirt in another person's eye while ignoring the plank in our own. He compared God's kingdom to finding a valuable pearl, laboring in a vineyard, or planting a crop. He observed the world around Him and used those observations to help people understand His message.

He observed people, too. He could readily see who was sincere and who was phony. He could tell whose heart was open to truth and whose was selfish and hard. The local religious leaders' attempts to deceive Him failed because He saw through their seemingly innocent questions. He met a Samaritan woman and instantly knew how desperately she wanted someone to love her and tell her she was a person of worth. And when a rich young man asked Him how to get into heaven, Jesus immediately saw that the man's wealth was an obstacle to his spiritual growth.

The Bible tells us people were amazed at Jesus' teachings. You and I may not dazzle anyone with our wisdom, but we can certainly follow Jesus' example by being keen observers of people, events, and situations around us.

Surely a part of wisdom is the ability to understand the meaning of what happens in our world. In order to understand it, we have to observe it first.

It's in the Book

A friend and I were talking recently about violence on TV and in movies. I said I believed that seeing violence in the media made it seem acceptable to young people and that it was probably a bad influence on them. He said he had read, on the other hand, that psychologists believe media violence enables people to "act out" their own violent tendencies in a harmless, fantasy-like way, which, in turn, may prevent them from actually committing acts of violence.

I don't know which of these views is right. I suspect in a few years another study of media violence will come out and present totally different conclusions. That's the trouble with contemporary "wisdom": It changes. There are experts today who tell us children need strict discipline, and also those who tell us to be lenient. Some people say "Be a pal to your child" while others say "Maintain your authority." It's a philosophical jungle out there.

The next generation's trendsetters will have a whole different set of ideas for rearing children, dealing with social and moral issues, and maintaining the balance of world power. If we pursue wisdom that reflects the current popular philosophy, we will be chasing a slippery quarry indeed!

> See to it that no one takes you captive through hollow and deceptive philosophy, which depends on human tradition and the basic principles of this world rather than on Christ (Colossians 2:8).

That brings us to the most important characteristic of Jesus' wisdom: It was centered on God's commandments. Jesus listened; He observed; and then He interpreted the things He saw and heard in light of the fundamental truths He knew. When Jesus faced choices, He didn't have

to check out the latest philosophical writings or
see which way the wind of popular opinion was
blowing. He had only to base His choices and
His actions on God's laws, which never change.

If we truly want to be wise—and working
mothers certainly need to be—I believe that we,
too, must anchor our wisdom in those principles
which have served seekers of wisdom well for
thousands of years. And God offers us an inex-
haustible source of timeless wisdom just for the
asking.

> "Therefore everyone who hears
> these words of mine and puts them
> into practice is like a wise man who
> built his house on the rock. The rain
> came down, the streams rose, and
> the winds blew and beat against that
> house; yet it did not fall, because it
> had its foundation on the rock. But
> everyone who hears these words of
> mine and does not put them into prac-
> tice is like a foolish man who built his
> house on sand. The rain came down,
> the streams rose, and the winds blew
> and beat against that house, and it
> fell with a great crash." When Jesus
> had finished saying these things, the
> crowds were amazed at his teach-
> ing. . . .
>
> (Matthew 7:24-28.)

Dear Reader:

We would appreciate hearing from you regarding this Harvest House pocket book. It will enable us to continue to give you the best in Christian publishing.

1. What most influenced you to purchase *Lifesavers for Working Mothers*?
   - ☐ Author
   - ☐ Subject matter
   - ☐ Backcover copy
   - ☐ Recommended
   - ☐ Cover/Title
   - ☐ _____

2. Your overall rating of this book:
   ☐ Excellent ☐ Very good ☐ Good ☐ Fair ☐ Poor

3. How likely would you be to purchase other books by this author?
   - ☐ Very likely
   - ☐ Somewhat likely
   - ☐ Not very likely
   - ☐ Not at all

4. After reading this Harvest House Pocket Book would you be inclined to purchase the complete book, *The Working Mother's Guide to Sanity*?
   ☐ Yes ☐ No

5. What types of books most interest you? (check all that apply)
   - ☐ Women's Books
   - ☐ Marriage Books
   - ☐ Current Issues
   - ☐ Self Help/Psychology
   - ☐ Bible Studies
   - ☐ Fiction
   - ☐ Biographies
   - ☐ Children's Books
   - ☐ Youth Books
   - ☐ Other _____

6. Please check the box next to your age group.
   - ☐ Under 18
   - ☐ 18-24
   - ☐ 25-34
   - ☐ 35-44
   - ☐ 45-54
   - ☐ 55 and over

   Mail to: Editorial Director
   Harvest House Publishers
   1075 Arrowsmith
   Eugene, OR 97402

Name _____

Address _____

City _____ State _____ Zip _____

**Thank you for helping us to help you
in future publications!**